Crabtree Publishing Company

PMB 16A 350 Fifth Avenue
Suite 3308
New York, NY 10118

612 Welland Avenue
St. Catharines,
Ontario L2M 5V6
www.crabtreebooks.com

Cataloging in Publication Data
Williams, Andy.
Oceans / Andy Williams
p. cm. -- (Nature Unfolds)
Contents: Broad ocean fold-out -- Tropical coasts -- The wide
ocean -- Continental slope -- Cool coastal waters -- Key to
foldout -- Deep ocean contents -- Deep ocean fold-out -- The
bright surface -- Twilight zone -- Deep abyss -- Deep ocean floor
-- Key to fold-out.
ISBN 0-7787-0310-X (RHC) -- ISBN 0-7787-0322-3 (pbk.)
1. Marine biology--Juvenile literature. 2. Ocean--Juvenile
literature. [1. Ocean. 2. Marine biology.] I. Camm, Martin, ill.
1. Title. III. Series.
QH91.16 .W545 2003
578.77--dc21
2002011422
LC

Coordinating Editor: **Ellen Rodger**
Project Editor: **Carrie Gleason**
Production Coordinator: **Rosie Gowsell**

Art and Editorial Direction: **Peter Sackett**
Editor: **Norman Barrett**
Designer: **Paul Richards, Designers & Partners**

Color Separation:

SC (Sang Choy) International Pte Ltd, Singapore

Printed and bound by
Sirivatana Interprint Public Co. Ltd.

OCEANS

NATURE UNFOLDS

ANDY WILLIAMS

—— *Illustrated by* ——

MARTIN CAMM

NATURE UNFOLDS

OCEANS

BROAD OCEAN

CONTENTS

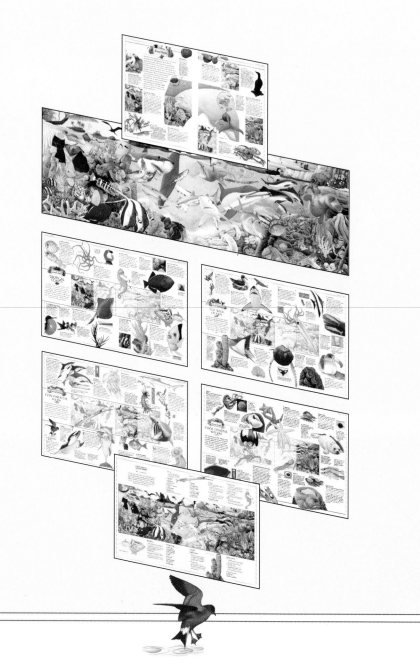

DEEP OCEAN

C O N T E N T S

Broad Ocean

About 60 percent of our planet is covered in water. The Atlantic Ocean is the second largest ocean and lies between North and South America and Europe. From the warm tropical waters of the Caribbean, the Atlantic Ocean opens to the vast darkness of the deep **abyss**. Nearing the European continent, the rocky **continental slope** begins to form, finally giving way to the cool waters of the western European coasts. Hidden under the water are mountains taller than Mount Everest, vast canyons that dwarf the Grand Canyon, and volcanoes constantly erupting at the bottom of the ocean. The Atlantic Ocean is home to an assortment of life. Among the colorful **coral reefs** and shallow waters of the tropical coasts, a variety of sea life is found. Every part of the ocean is home to some form of marine life.

▲ RESTING POINTS
Many species of seabirds fly around the oceans for months, transferring pollen and seeds as they stop off at the many islands. Some seabirds travel thousands of miles before returning to their nests.

▼ SEED DISPERSAL
Ocean **currents**, wind, and animals carry seeds and pollen across the oceans. Coconuts that fall into the sea in the Caribbean may arrive on a beach in Europe years later. The next time you find a branch on the beach, think about where it might have come from.

Warm water

◄ TROPICAL COASTS
The tropical coasts have warm, clear blue or turquoise water. Coral reefs in the shallow waters teem with fish and other life. These reefs take thousands of years to grow. Some of the most brightly colored fish live among the stinging **tentacles** of **anemones**. In the **coral** are "cleaning stations," where small fish eat waste food and **parasites** off larger fish and sharks. Tropical water temperatures are between 68°F (20°C) in the winter and 104°F (40°C) in shallow lagoons in the summer.

◄ FOOD CHAIN
Plankton is the name given to small animals and plants that drift around the world's oceans. Plankton cannot swim. There are two types, phytoplankton (plants) and zooplankton (animals). Plankton are essential to life in the oceans, providing food for the small fish, jellyfish, and other animals near the bottom of the **food chain**.

THE WIDE OCEAN ➤
The deepest part of the ocean is a cold dark place where the water temperature never rises above 39°F (4°C). At the surface of the ocean, there are few **nutrients** and little life. Animals that live here are expert hunters. In these waters are some of the fastest fish on earth. Birds glide above the water's surface, looking for food.

CONTINENTAL SLOPE ➤

The area where the **seabed** rises from the deep abyss to the shallow coastal waters is called the continental slope. The continental slope is rich with marine life compared to the open ocean. The deep ocean water, rich in nutrients, creates a "soup" of food for **algae** to grow, and this in turn brings small fish, jellyfish, and other marine life, right up the food chain to larger fish and **marine mammals**.

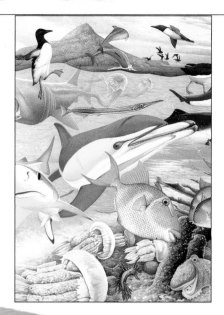

POLLUTION ➤

The oceans support a great deal of animal and plant life, but the water and the life in them are fragile. Pollution threatens life in the ocean. Oil that spills from ships or is dumped into the ocean and sticks to the feathers of seabirds, drowning or poisoning them as they try to clean themselves. Poisons in the oil build up in the food chain and cause **predators** such as whales, dolphins, birds, and sharks to become ill or die.

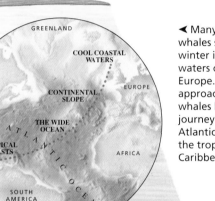

◄ Many humpback whales spend the winter in the cool waters off northern Europe. As winter approaches, the whales begin a long journey across the Atlantic Ocean to the tropical Caribbean.

▼ COOL COASTAL WATERS

The continental shelf is shallow compared with the deep water in the open ocean. **Shoals** of fish, large numbers of birds, and abundant seaweed live in shallow water. The waters along the European coasts are cool all year compared with tropical coasts. The water temperature ranges from 41°F (5°C) in the winter to 68°F (20°C) in the summer. Coastal water is the water closest to land.

Cold water

Mid-Atlantic ridge

DRIFTING OASES ➤

The open ocean is not rich with food and offers little **camouflage**, so patches of seaweed are like oases in the desert. Fish, turtles, sharks, and seabirds gather together on and around large areas of a type of seaweed called sargassum.

◄ WEB BURRFISH

The web burrfish is a porcupine fish. It gets its name from the sharp spines along its body. The web burrfish puffs up its body when threatened by predators. The web burrfish is almost impossible for predators to eat because of its size and sharp spines that stick out when it is inflated.

➤ The royal tern preys on fish and other marine life.

◄ BRITTLE-STAR

The brittle-star is a **starfish** with long, gangly arms that break off easily. Brittle-stars are found in both cool and warm waters. They gather together in large **colonies** on rocky coasts with fast-moving currents.

Broad Ocean

TROPICAL COASTS

The shallow coastal waters of the **tropics** thrive with sea life. The coral reefs in the tropical coasts take thousands of years to grow. The reefs are home to a countless variety of colorful fish and other animals. As reefs die and break down, they are ground down by the wind and the waves into very small particles that create white sandy coral beaches.

▼ MAGNIFICENT FRIGATEBIRD

Named after a ship, frigatebirds glide through the air looking for other species of seabird. When the frigatebird spots another bird fishing, it tries to steal its catch. Frigatebirds look like **prehistoric** animals as they soar high over the coastline with their pterodactyl-like wings. The male frigatebird has a bright red or orange throat that it can blow up like a balloon during **courtship**.

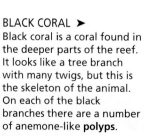

▲ Once another bird catches a fish, it is continually attacked by the frigatebird until the fish is released.

SOUTHERN STINGRAY ➤

The southern stingray has two spines on its tail that deliver a painful, but not fatal, sting to swimmers. Once stung, the swimmer may be paralyzed until the poison wears off. Stingrays cruise the seabed looking for their prey of shellfish.

BLACK CORAL ➤

Black coral is a coral found in the deeper parts of the reef. It looks like a tree branch with many twigs, but this is the skeleton of the animal. On each of the black branches there are a number of anemone-like **polyps**.

▲ The stingray tail has a barbed tip, like a fish-hook. The tail breaks off to allow the stingray to escape danger.

◄ ROYAL TERN

The royal tern is a small bird with slim, sharp wings. When flying, the royal tern points its orange bill at prey in the water. Its legs are usually black, but are sometimes orange, like its bill. The royal tern looks after its young for as long as five months after they hatch, which is longer than most other terns.

BIGEYE ➤

The bigeye gets its name from its large eyes, which it uses to see in the dark. The bigeye searches for its food of small fish and **larvae** at night. Bigeyes are found around rocky sea bottoms or in among the coral.

▼ BLACK DURGEON

The black durgeon belongs to the triggerfish **family**. Black durgeons have sharp spines that, once raised, are locked in place to jam itself in a nook and prevent it being removed by a predator. If eaten, the spines stick in the mouth of a predator, causing the predator to spit out the fish.

◄ SEAHORSE

The seahorse is a small fish that has a horse-like head and swims upright. The female lays about one hundred eggs, then passes them to the male. The male nurtures the eggs in a pouch on its body for a month or more before they hatch.

The sharp dorsal spines of the black durgeon.

▼ NASSAU GROUPER

Nassau groupers are very large slow-swimming fish. They live in crevices and other nooks around rocky ledges, reefs, and shipwrecks. Groupers compete for the same food as sharks and barracudas, because of their similar size and shared habitat. Nassau groupers have to be careful not to become the shark's dinner themselves.

▼ BANDED BUTTERFLY FISH

The black-and-white striped banded butterfly fish lives among the coral and on rocky reefs. It is usually found alone or with one other banded butterfly fish. These fish have a small delicate beak that they use to feed on the soft coral polyps.

◄ FAIRY BASSLET

The colorful fairy basslet is a small fish found among the ledges, caves, and rocky outcrops around reef areas. This fish keeps its belly toward the nearest rocky surface. When at the top of a cave or under a ledge, this fish is usually upside-down!

ROCK BEAUTY ➤

Rock beauties live among rocks and shells and on coral reefs to depths of 300 feet (100 m). This colorful little fish stays close to its home, rarely traveling more than a few feet from safety. The sharp outer edges of its **gill slits** (bottom right) protect it from predators.

◄ BROWN PELICAN

Pelicans circle overhead looking for fish or sit on boats and posts. They have a large pouch under their bill. When the pelican dives into the water, its pouch fills with water and fish. The pelican then spits the water out and is left with the fish, which it quickly eats.

▲ RED-FOOTED BOOBY

The red-footed booby soars across the wave tops even in rough weather. Red-footed boobies nest on rocky ledges and islands. They dive deep to catch their prey, piercing the water at high speed like an arrow, often popping up to sit on the surface with a fish in their mouth.

◄ GREAT WHITE SHARK

Despite its reputation, the great white shark attacks and kills fewer people than the tiger shark. Great whites roam the open ocean and coastal areas. Their dark upper side makes it difficult for seals, their main food, to see them against the dark sea floor.

Broad Ocean

THE WIDE OCEAN

Crossing the Atlantic Ocean means leaving the shallow coastal waters teeming with life and passing through a wide open expanse of water. In the wide ocean, giant marine animals **migrate** from northern feeding grounds to warm breeding grounds. Large shoals of fish find safety in massive numbers. Large and small predators patrol the clear blue water waiting for any opportunity to feed.

TRUMPET SPONGES ►

Sponges are animals without heads, limbs, or **internal organs**. Sponges live underwater attached to rocks or plants. Large, soft trumpet sponges gather together in small colonies, looking like factory smoke stacks. The sponges are home to many species of small fish that feed on the millions of tiny eggs produced by the sponges.

▲ SPOTTED EAGLE RAY

The spotted eagle **ray** soars through the clear blue waters of the tropics, flapping its "wings" like a bird. When feeding, the spotted eagle ray rests on the seabed and uses its wings to suck small clams from the muddy bottom.

▼ SEA FAN CORAL

Sea fan corals are large corals with soft **tissue** around a chalky skeleton. They often live alone around the base of, or just away from, a coral reef. Many species of sea fan coral have a broad fan-like structure that sways back and forth as the current passes through it. Other species have tree-like branches.

SQUID ▾

Squid are found in all of the world's oceans in groups of thousands. Squid are the primary diet of many whale and dolphin species. Squid have thin bodies that allow them to swim very fast.

▾ Squid have a sharp parrot-like beak hidden in the middle of their tentacles.

◄ ▲ Small fish often tug on the tip of the Moorish idol's long dorsal fin.

MOORISH IDOL ➤
The brightly colored Moorish idol has a long flowing **dorsal fin** that flicks back from its head. It has a long snout with tweezer-like jaws.

▾ ANCHOVY

The anchovy is a small fish. **Schools** of anchovy contain tens of thousands of fish. Anchovy have a shiny, silvery skin that shimmers in the sunlight just below the surface of the water. When they move, anchovies look like a large flock of birds swimming together. It is not only other fish that catch and eat anchovies, people also eat them.

▾ HAWKSBILL TURTLE
The hawksbill turtle has a hooked bill that it uses to get into small crevices and remove fish and crabs, which it then eats. The hawksbill turtle has a beautiful swirling pattern on its shell. Turtles breathe air, so they need to spend some time at the surface.

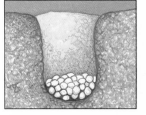

▲ Every two or three years the female turtle returns to the same beach on which it was born and lays eggs in a nest dug in the sand.

◄ HUMPBACK WHALE
Humpback whales are found throughout the northern Atlantic Ocean. They migrate to colder Arctic waters in the summer and to the Caribbean and islands off Africa in the winter. Their huge **pectoral fins** help identify them as they leap high into the air. Humpbacks have a distinctive "call" or music.

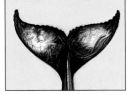

▲ Scientists identify individual whales by the patterns on the underside of their tails.

◄ GIANT CLAM
Giant clams are large shellfish that lie on the bottom of the seabed and among the rocks of a coral reef. Giant clams grow up to three feet (1 m) in diameter. Algae often grow at the edge of the shell, giving it a colorful appearance.

COMMON DOLPHIN ➤

Common dolphins have bodies that are **streamlined**. Their bodies have a yellow and white hourglass pattern, but the colors vary a little in each dolphin. Common dolphins feed on fish and squid. After their young are born, common dolphins gather together in groups of thousands to protect them. When common dolphins are around, their high-pitched whistles can be heard by people on ships and boats.

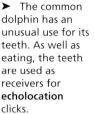

➤ The common dolphin has an unusual use for its teeth. As well as eating, the teeth are used as receivers for **echolocation** clicks.

▲ Common dolphins have long slender jaws filled with up to 120 sharp, pointed teeth.

UMBRELLA JELLYFISH ➤

The umbrella jellyfish does not have long stinging tentacles like other species of jellyfish. It has eight thick tentacles hanging below its dome and emerging from a cauliflower-looking mass. The tentacles produce a sticky oily mucus that traps plankton, which is then eaten by the tentacles.

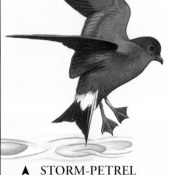

Broad Ocean

CONTINENTAL SLOPE

In the oceans, around the continents, there are shelves, slopes, and rises that make up what is called the continental margins. Continental slopes extend off the continental shelves. The slopes gently grade down from the seashore at depths of 350 feet (100 m). The slope waters are rich in sea life. Sea plants grow and fish, sharks, and dolphins thrive in these waters.

GARFISH ➤

The long slender garfish is difficult to see as it speeds through the water, because its shimmering silver color camouflages it against the surface. The garfish has very powerful jaws packed with sharp teeth.

▲ STORM-PETREL (BLACK)

The storm-petrel is a small bird that seems to tiptoe across the water, beating their wings hard to keep themselves up. They feed in the open ocean on plankton and small fish.

BOTTLENOSE DOLPHIN ➤

Bottlenose dolphins get their name from their thick, blunt nose. They are one of the largest dolphin species, growing to 13 feet (4 m) long. When a calf is born, its mother helps it to the surface and supports it while it takes its first few breaths. The calf and mother rely on other members of the pod for help.

▲ GUILLEMOT

Guillemots are small birds that nest on rocky ledges. Their young throw themselves off the cliff when they are ready to fly. Guillemots feed on small fish close to the surface. They dive under, then beat their wings, so it appears that they are flying underwater.

BLUE SHARK ➤

The blue shark patrols the open ocean, keeping a sharp lookout for food with its large, round black eyes. It gets its name from the silver-blue color of its streamlined body. The blue shark glides through the water, eating fish such as herring and mackerel, with its long pectoral fins outstretched.

▲ Blue sharks have sharp, pointed teeth.

SEA SLUG (COASTAL) ➤

Sea slugs get their name because they look like land slugs. They have long tentacles on their heads. The coastal sea slug patrols the water to about 130 feet (40 m) deep, feeding on tiny animals.

▲ Jerky swimming movement of the sea slug.

◄ PLANKTON

Plankton is the term used to describe plants and animals that cannot swim through the water but travel with the currents. Plankton is made up of drifting seaweed, tiny animals, and even fish eggs. Plankton is essential for all life in the oceans. It is the first step in the food chain.

◄ BASKING SHARK

Basking sharks are giants of the shark family. Only the whale shark is bigger. Basking sharks grow up to 36 feet (11 m) in length and weigh as much as 11,000 pounds (5,000 kg). They are not a threat to divers or swimmers. Basking sharks graze on plankton, using their specialized gills to filter the food from the water.

LION'S MANE JELLYFISH ➤

Many jellyfish do not harm people, but the lion's mane jellyfish delivers a very painful sting. The largest jellyfish in the world, the lion's mane jellyfish has tentacles that grow up to 100 feet (30 m) long. Lion's mane jellyfish are found drifting in the open ocean, capturing small fish and plankton in their tentacles. The eggs of the lion's main jellyfish are produced and developed in the tail. In the spring, they detach as small jellyfish.

▼▲ A triggerfish feeding off a cluster of mussels (above) and using its locking mechanism to wedge itself into a rock crevice (below).

▲ GRAY TRIGGERFISH

There are many species of triggerfish. The gray triggerfish is found in coastal areas to depths of 330 feet (100 m). Using their powerful jaws and sharp teeth, triggerfish crush the shells of their prey. Their first dorsal fin has a sharp spine that locks in place. It is unlocked by the trigger, or second spine of its dorsal fin.

➤ A lion's mane jellyfish stings and entangles its prey before eating it.

KELP ➤

Kelp, a type of seaweed, grows on rocky shores and on the seabed. Kelp anchors itself to the rocks or seabed by a series of roots. The **fronds** of the kelp extend from the top of the trunk and grow up to 165 feet (50 m) long in some species.

◄ EDIBLE SEA URCHIN

The edible **sea urchin** has very short spines. It eats algae and kelp.

PUFFIN ➤

Sitting on the surface of the water in summer, puffins look like guillemots, except for their colorful beaks. Puffins build nests in burrows on isolated islands, and this makes them prey to ground-living predators such as rats and cats.

▼ Puffins dive into the waves to capture sand eels from below.

Broad Ocean

COOL COASTAL WATERS

The cool waters along the coasts are filled with a variety of sea life. Animals along the shore compete for space. As the tides come in and go out, areas of the shore are covered with water, then exposed to air. Starfish and sea slugs live in vast forests of **kelp** just off the shore. The kelp provides food and shelter for small fish. Seals swim off the rocky shores, which are covered with cockles and limpets.

▼ HARBOR PORPOISE

The harbor porpoise is the smallest member of the whale and dolphin family living in the **northern hemisphere**. It has a small triangular dorsal fin, but shows very little of itself at the surface. Porpoises are found near the coastline.

▲ POLLACK

Pollack are silver colored fish found from the shore to depths of 800 feet (250 m). They rest in gullies and around shipwrecks, watching for small fish and sand eels with their large eyes.

3

▲ Porpoises' spade-like teeth allow them to hold large fish in their mouth.

▼ GREATER SPOTTED DOGFISH

The greater spotted, or nursehound, dogfish is a small member of the shark family that spends its life close to the seabed. Like most sharks, dogfish are not a threat to people. Dogfish feed on small fish, crabs, and shrimp. They lay their eggs in shallow water, the horny cases (1) tangled among the kelp. The young develop over five to eleven months (2). The egg cases they leave behind are called mermaids' purses (3).

2   **1**

▼ STARFISH

All starfish have at least five arms radiating from a central body, and are able to regrow any arms they lose. The red cushionstar (top) is a small starfish that has five short arms and is found among kelp forests. The larger, seven-armed starfish (bottom) lives close to the shelf edge and moves quickly using its long tube-like feet. The Bloody Henry starfish (middle) feeds on plankton.

▲ LUMPSUCKER

The lumpsucker clings to rocks in fast-moving currents using the sucker-like fins on its belly. These fish live in deeper offshore waters, but come into shallow water to lay their eggs, which the male then guards.

▼ GRAY SEAL

The gray seal lives around rocky coasts and swims among the kelp forest. Like other marine mammals, seals have the same bones as mammals and their flippers look like small arms and legs. The young are called pups and are born with white coats. The pups cannot swim until they have **molted** their coat.

▼ The pups have very large, watery eyes. Seal pups "cry" when they are left on the rocks by their mother, and this helps her find them.

▼ CUCKOO WRASSE

Male cuckoo wrasse have a blue head, and the females have a reddish-colored body. Some of the females turn into males after the age of seven. The new male then finds its own **territory** and tries to encourage females to join him.

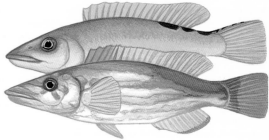

▶ Octopus eyes look like human eyes.

LIMPETS ▶

These two species of limpet attach themselves to rocks close to shore. The larger, common limpet changes sex when it is four years old, while the smaller, tortoiseshell limpet stays the same sex throughout its life.

▲ CURLED OCTOPUS

Octopus have eight tentacles, each with powerful suckers to grip onto the rocks or their prey. To move quickly, an octopus squirts bursts of water from inside its body cavity through a funnel. The funnel can be bent, so the octopus can move in any direction.

▼ WOLF-FISH

The wolf-fish lurks in the darker waters between rocks, watching and waiting for its prey to come by. Wolf-fish have very strong jaws with dog-like teeth that they use to crush open the shells of crabs and mussels. Wolf-fish grow new teeth to replace teeth that get broken or worn down. They lay their eggs in a mound and curl their body around them to give them protection.

Broad Ocean

KEY TO FOLD-OUT

Use these key numbers if you want to identify the
animals and plants on the Broad Ocean fold-out.
Most of them are featured on pages 12-19, and they
are listed here in bold type. Plants and animals that
are not featured are also keyed and listed here,
with a brief description.

5 Fire Coral
Fire coral is a large stinging coral. A sting
from a fire coral causes swelling and pain
in swimmers and divers.
6 **Fairy Basslet**
7 **Seahorse**
8 **Web Burrfish**
9 **Southern Stingray**
10 **Royal Tern**
11 **Magnificent Frigatebird**
12 **Bigeye**
13 **Nassau Grouper**
14 **Black Coral**
15 **Black Durgeon**
16 **Brittle-Star**
17 **Trumpet Sponges**

Nassau grouper (13)

1 **Rock Beauty**
2 Barsnout Goby
The barsnout goby is found around the
tops of corals. It is one of the "cleaner"
fish of the coral reef, cleaning parasites
from larger fish.
3 **Banded Butterfly Fish**
4 Bleached Coral
When bleached coral dies, the soft flesh
dies away, leaving only the chalky white
skeleton behind. Pollution, changes in
water temperature, or a drop in sea
level all kill the coral.

18 **Moorish Idol**
19 **Spotted Eagle Ray**
20 **Red-Footed Booby**
21 **Great White Shark**
22 **Hawksbill Turtle**
23 **Squid**
24 **Sea Fan Coral**
25 **Giant Clam**
26 **Anchovy**
27 **Humpback Whale**
28 **Brown Pelican**
29 **Guillemot**
30 **Basking Shark**
31 **Plankton**
32 **Blue Shark**

Deep Ocean

Traveling from the surface to the bottom of the Atlantic Ocean takes a very long time. The deepest parts of the ocean reach a depth of six miles (10 km). Different species of marine life exist deeper in the ocean than those at the surface. Animals in the lower layers of the ocean have adapted for life in the cold, dark depths. Oceans are home to some of the oldest animals on earth, for this is where life began. Scientists have only recently begun studying the deep ocean. They have discovered that it is like an alien world, with strange prehistoric creatures, animals that light up in the dark, and giant squid that lurk in the darkness of the depths.

▲ VOLCANIC ISLANDS

Volcanic islands appear and disappear with one eruption. They provide a resting place for seabirds in the middle of the ocean. Some volcanic islands have very steep sides that plunge to the bottom of the ocean. Underwater, these steep sides provide a refuge for sea life.

▶ THE BRIGHT SURFACE

In the upper layer of the deep ocean, marine life is scarce compared to the lower layers. Animals in the top 3,600 feet (1,100 m) take advantage of any food that comes along, and prey species try to avoid being eaten. The fastest swimming fish live at the surface.

▶ THE UNKNOWN

Ocean scientists are just starting to learn how many animals exist in the oceans. Beaked whales (below) are one of the least understood species of whale, and more species are being discovered by scientists every few years.

▶ TWILIGHT ZONE

Below the surface, light cannot pass through the water. The twilight zone is the area where very little light reaches. Only animals with specially adapted eyes can see. Some animals look upward toward the surface to silhouette their prey against the light. The only green plants in the twilight zone are those that grew in the upper layers and then sank down.

NIGHT AND DAY ▶
At sunset, many animals from lower ocean layers, such as jellyfish and squid, migrate to the brighter moonlit layers. This upward movement means a rise of thousands of feet.

Garfish (36)

33 Umbrella Jellyfish
34 Sea Slug (coastal)
35 Common Dolphin
36 Garfish
37 Lion's Mane Jellyfish
38 Bottlenose Dolphin
39 Storm-Petrel (Black)
40 Gray Triggerfish
41 Curled Octopus
42 Wolf-Fish
43 Puffin

49 Sunset Cup Coral
The brightly colored sunset cup coral is found in north European waters, on gullies and overhanging rocks.
50 Dead Men's Fingers
Dead men's fingers is a species of soft coral. The short, dumpy lobes of the coral reminded early sailors of the fingers of dead men.
51 Cuckoo Wrasse (male)
52 Red Cushionstar
53 Sea Slug (skirted)
The skirted sea slug is brightly colored, long, and slender. It lives close to shore

around north European coasts. Its "skirt" is a feature of this family of sea slugs.
54 Bloody Henry Starfish
55 Branching Sponge
The branching sponge has branches growing out from a central trunk.
56 Gray Seal
57 Kelp
58 Herring Gull
The large herring gull wanders around quaysides and circles over the seashore making its pleading cry.
59 Limpet, Common

Seahorse (7)

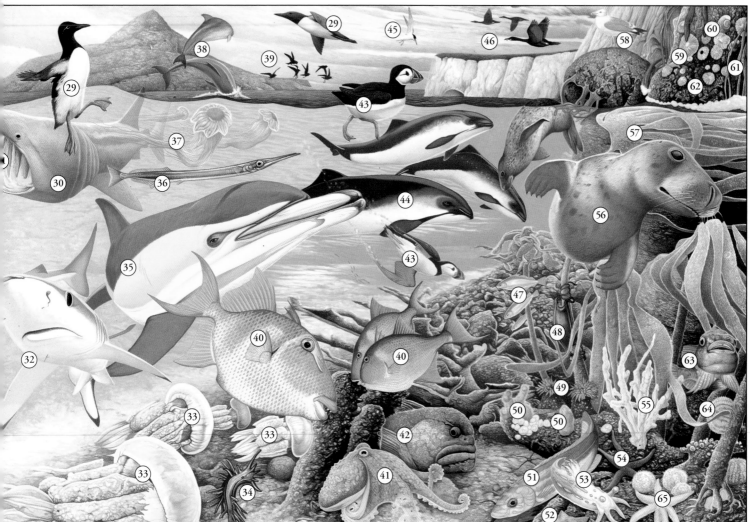

44 Harbor Porpoise
45 Little Tern
The little tern hovers low over the water surface, furiously beating its wings. When it spots a small fish, it rises slightly before plunging into the water.
46 Great Cormorant
The great cormorant is a black, long-necked bird that is a good swimmer, and surface-dives to find its prey. Cormorants perch on posts and buoys with their wings outstretched to dry.
47 Pollack
48 Greater Spotted Dogfish (egg case)

Trumpet Sponges (17)

60 Periwinkle
The periwinkle lives in weedy coastal areas and is the small spiral-shaped shell commonly found on the shore.
61 Channeled Wrack
The tough, strap-like channeled wrack is a seaweed that has channels along its fronds, creating a gutter. It is found in large groups just below the high-water mark.
62 Limpet, Tortoiseshell
63 Lumpsucker
64 Edible Sea Urchin
65 Seven-Armed Starfish

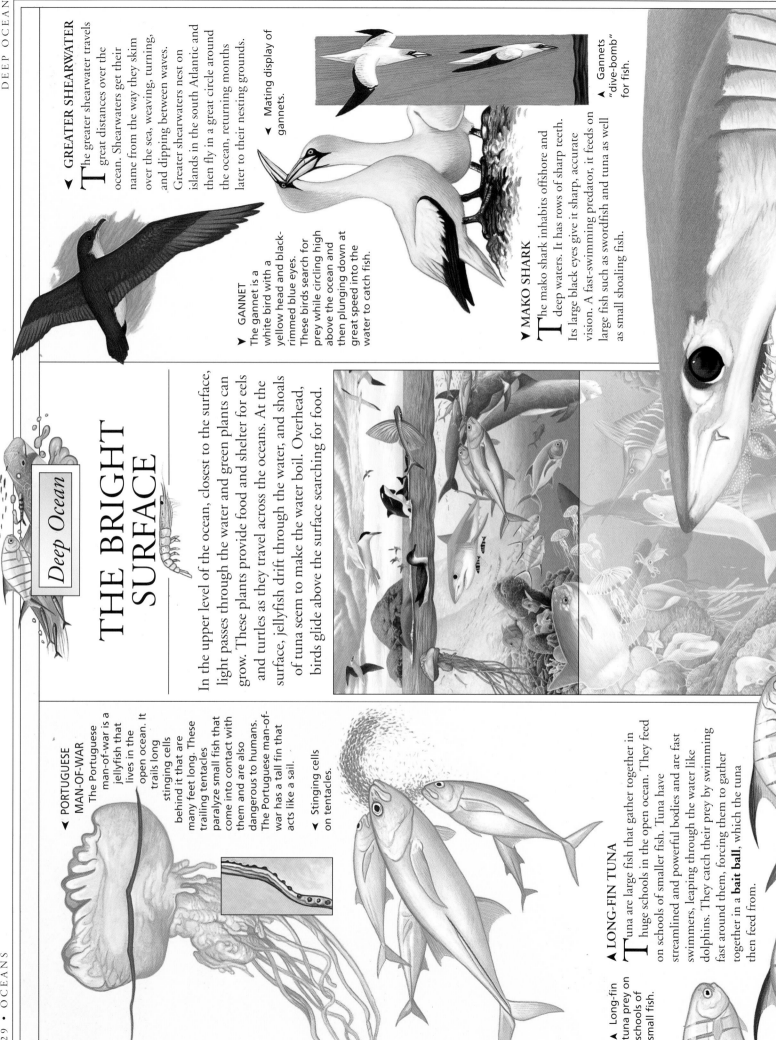

GREATER SHEARWATER

The greater shearwater travels great distances over the ocean. Shearwaters get their name from the way they skim over the sea, weaving, turning, and dipping between waves. Greater shearwaters nest on islands in the south Atlantic and then fly in a great circle around the ocean, returning months later to their nesting grounds.

▼ Mating display of gannets.

▼ GANNET
The gannet is a white bird with a yellow head and black-rimmed blue eyes. These birds search for prey while circling high above the ocean and then plunging down at great speed into the water to catch fish.

▲ Gannets "dive-bomb" for fish.

▼ MAKO SHARK

The mako shark inhabits offshore and deep waters. It has rows of sharp teeth. Its large black eyes give it sharp, accurate vision. A fast-swimming predator, it feeds on large fish such as swordfish and tuna as well as small shoaling fish.

Deep Ocean

THE BRIGHT SURFACE

In the upper level of the ocean, closest to the surface, light passes through the water and green plants can grow. These plants provide food and shelter for eels and turtles as they travel across the oceans. At the surface, jellyfish drift through the water, and shoals of tuna seem to make the water boil. Overhead, birds glide above the surface searching for food.

▼ PORTUGUESE MAN-OF-WAR
The Portuguese man-of-war is a jellyfish that lives in the open ocean. It trails long stinging cells behind it that are many feet long. These trailing tentacles paralyze small fish that come into contact with them and are also dangerous to humans. The Portuguese man-of-war has a tall fin that acts like a sail.

▼ Stinging cells on tentacles.

▲ LONG-FIN TUNA

Tuna are large fish that gather together in huge schools in the open ocean. They feed on schools of smaller fish. Tuna have streamlined and powerful bodies and are fast swimmers, leaping through the water like dolphins. They catch their prey by swimming fast around them, forcing them to gather together in a **bait ball**, which the tuna then feed from.

▲ Long-fin tuna prey on schools of small fish.

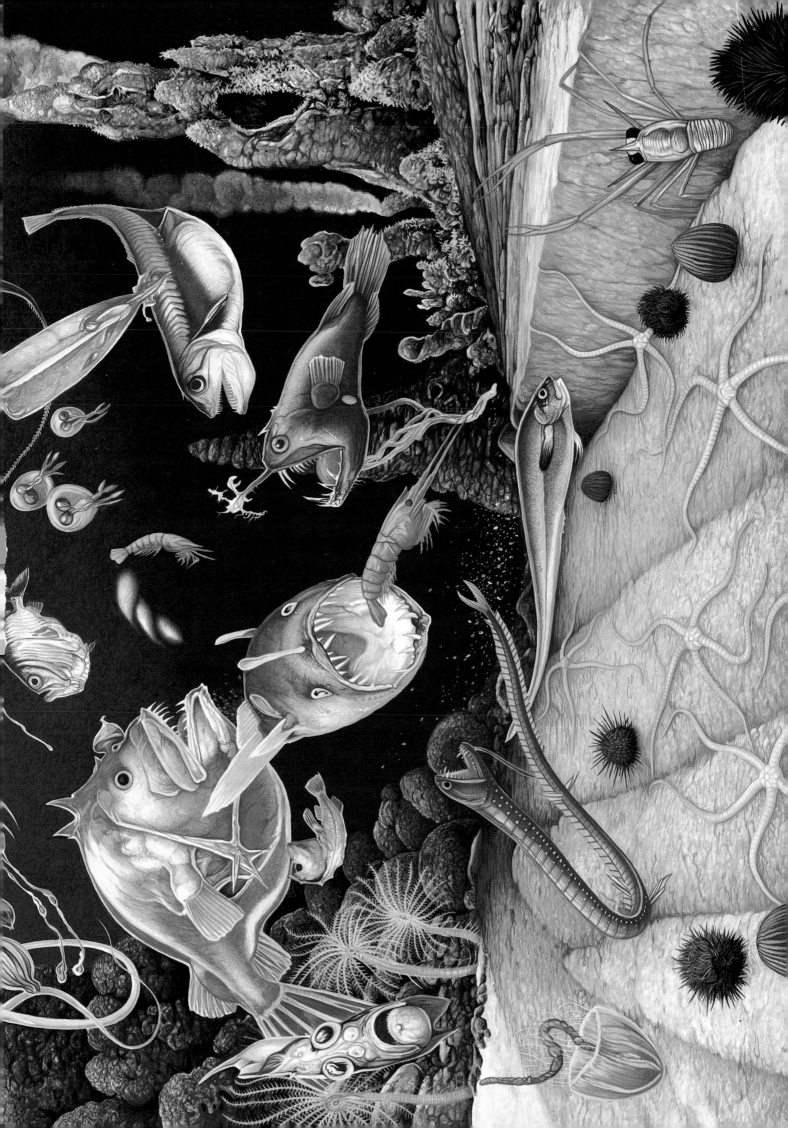

Black Smokers

▶ DEEP ABYSS

The deep abyss is the part of the ocean where sunlight does not reach. Some of the animals that live in this cold dark place produce their own light. In the deep abyss, sperm whales dive down into the deep to hunt giant squid. Their loud clicks create echoes. Strange fish hang motionless in the water, waiting for prey to come within range.

▶ LUMINESCENCE

Some fish, such as angler-fish and lantern fish, have developed special **cells** or live with types of **bacteria** in their bodies that produce light. The light is useful in parts of the ocean where natural light cannot reach.

▲ DEEP OCEAN FLOOR

Years ago, it was thought that the deep ocean floor was empty and rocky. Now, thanks to deep-sea submarines, we know that life does exist at the bottom of the ocean. On the ocean floor, many animals rely on the large amounts of food that sink to the bottom from the animals and plants that die above it.

Hot Vents

Oceanic Crust

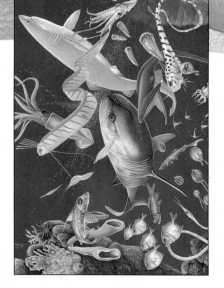

▼ RECYCLING

Dead animals sink to the sea bottom. The **carcass** of a large marine animal provides food for sea-bed fish for many months. As the carcass **decays**, small pieces are carried by the deep ocean currents to the continental slope, even reaching the upper ocean to provide food for plankton.

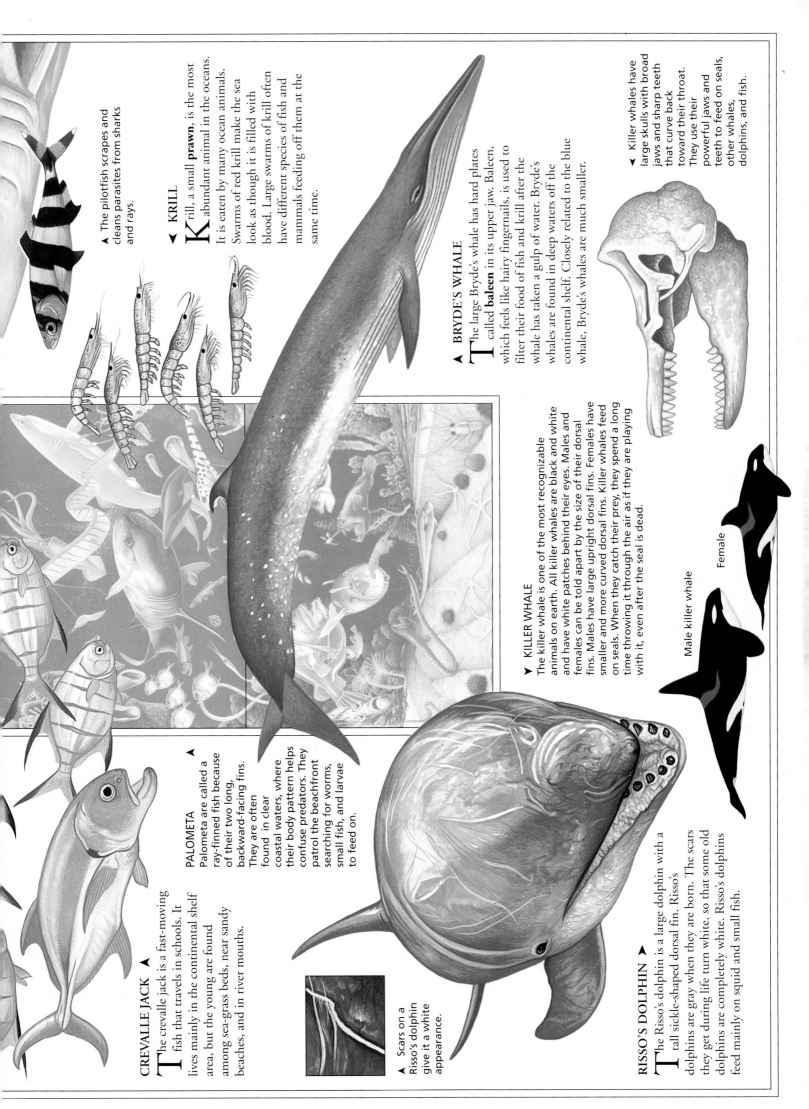

▲ The pilotfish scrapes and cleans parasites from sharks and rays.

▼ KRILL

Krill, a small **prawn**, is the most abundant animal in the oceans. It is eaten by many ocean animals. Swarms of red krill make the sea look as though it is filled with blood. Large swarms of krill often have different species of fish and mammals feeding off them at the same time.

▲ BRYDE'S WHALE

The large Bryde's whale has hard plates called **baleen** in its upper jaw. Baleen, which feels like hairy fingernails, is used to filter their food of fish and krill after the whale has taken a gulp of water. Bryde's whales are found in deep waters off the continental shelf. Closely related to the blue whale, Bryde's whales are much smaller.

▼ Killer whales have large skulls with broad jaws and sharp teeth that curve back toward their throat. They use their powerful jaws and teeth to feed on seals, other whales, dolphins, and fish.

▼ KILLER WHALE

The killer whale is one of the most recognizable animals on earth. All killer whales are black and white and have white patches behind their eyes. Males and females can be told apart by the size of their dorsal fins. Males have large upright dorsal fins. Females have smaller and more curved dorsal fins. Killer whales feed on seals. When they catch their prey, they spend a long time throwing it through the air as if they are playing with it, even after the seal is dead.

Male killer whale

Female

CREVALLE JACK ▲

The crevalle jack is a fast-moving fish that travels in schools. It lives mainly in the continental shelf area, but the young are found among sea-grass beds, near sandy beaches, and in river mouths.

PALOMETA ▲

Palometa are called a ray-finned fish because of their two long, backward-facing fins. They are often found in clear coastal waters, where their body pattern helps confuse predators. They patrol the beachfront searching for worms, small fish, and larvae to feed on.

▲ Scars on a Risso's dolphin give it a white appearance.

RISSO'S DOLPHIN ▶

The Risso's dolphin is a large dolphin with a tall sickle-shaped dorsal fin. Risso's dolphins are gray when they are born. The scars they get during life turn white, so that some old dolphins are completely white. Risso's dolphins feed mainly on squid and small fish.

► LEATHERBACK TURTLE

Leatherback turtles are the giants of the turtle family. They live in the open ocean. Leatherback turtles have soft mouths and feed mainly on jellyfish. The shell of the leatherback turtle does not have the bony plates that divide other turtle and tortoise shells into sections.

TRUMPET SPONGES ►

Trumpet sponges are found clinging to the sides of rocky ledges. This group of sponges comes in many different colors and shapes. Trumpet sponges provide food for ocean animals by producing clouds of eggs which are released into the sea.

► ATLANTIC TORPEDO RAY

Electric rays produce an electric current in the water. The electricity that the ray produces is used to stun small fish so that the ray can eat them. It also gives a shock to swimmers.

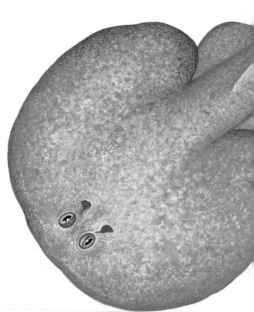

Deep Ocean

TWILIGHT ZONE

In the twilight zone, the bright surface and the dark, deep abyss meet. Some marine life found here migrate from deeper in the ocean during the night, while others dive from the surface to feed. In the twilight zone, sponges cling to rocks that rise from the deep, and sperm whales hunt giant squid from the deep abyss.

OCEAN SUNFISH ►

The ocean sunfish is shaped like a trash can lid with a pair of legs splayed out doing the splits. The sunfish travels slowly and is found in the deep ocean and around the coasts. As the sunfish swims through the water, its uppermost fin waves in the air. In many parts of the world, this fish is called the moonfish.

► Young sunfish have spines that protect them from predators.

▲ COMPASS JELLYFISH

The compass jellyfish has a ten inch (25 cm) diameter bell-shaped body. Its body is almost transparent, with brown lines from the center of the bell out to the edges, which look like the direction lines on a compass. Its tentacles are small compared with other species of jellyfish.

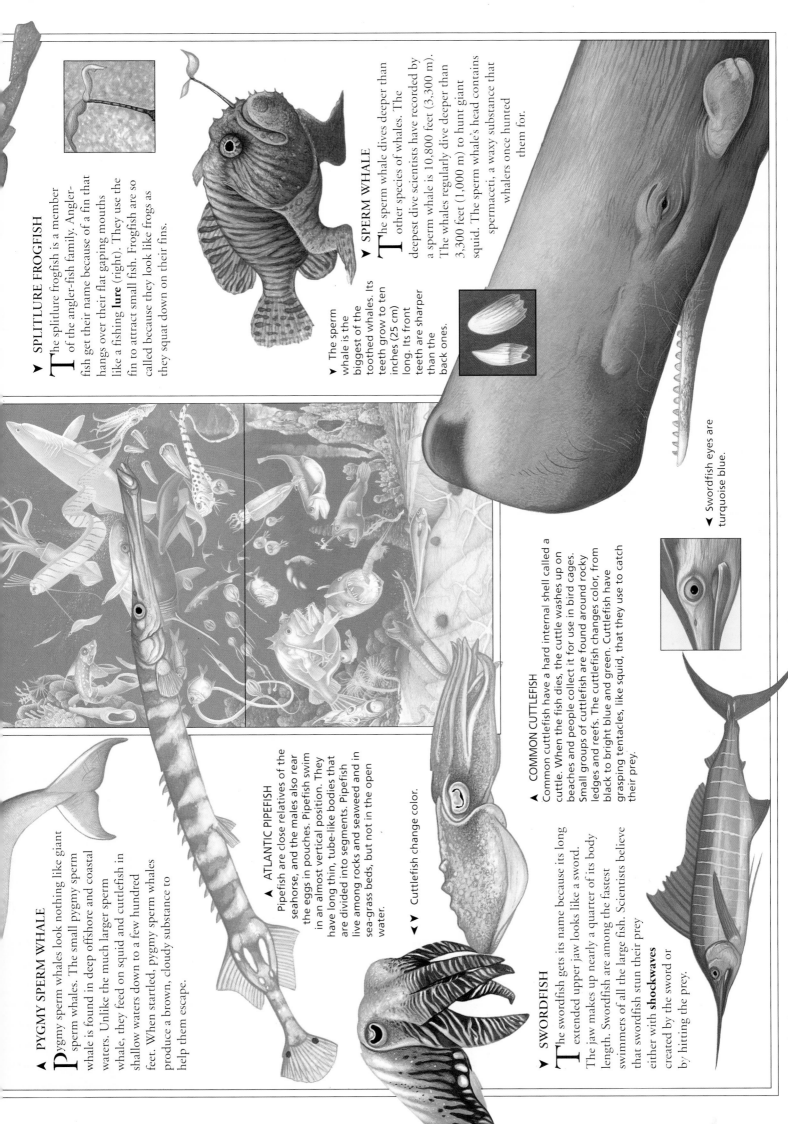

SPLITLURE FROGFISH

The splitlure frogfish is a member of the angler-fish family. Angler-fish get their name because of a fin that hangs over their flat gaping mouths like a fishing **lure** (right). They use the fin to attract small fish. Frogfish are so called because they look like frogs as they squat down on their fins.

SPERM WHALE

The sperm whale dives deeper than other species of whales. The deepest dive scientists have recorded by a sperm whale is 10,800 feet (3,300 m). The whales regularly dive deeper than 3,300 feet (1,000 m) to hunt giant squid. The sperm whale's head contains spermaceti, a waxy substance that whalers once hunted them for.

▶ The sperm whale is the biggest of the toothed whales. Its teeth grow to ten inches (25 cm) long. Its front teeth are sharper than the back ones.

▶ Swordfish eyes are turquoise blue.

PYGMY SPERM WHALE

Pygmy sperm whales look nothing like giant sperm whales. The small pygmy sperm whale is found in deep offshore and coastal waters. Unlike the much larger sperm whale, they feed on squid and cuttlefish in shallow waters down to a few hundred feet. When startled, pygmy sperm whales produce a brown, cloudy substance to help them escape.

ATLANTIC PIPEFISH

Pipefish are close relatives of the seahorse, and the males also rear the eggs in pouches. Pipefish swim in an almost vertical position. They have long thin, tube-like bodies that are divided into segments. Pipefish live among rocks and seaweed and in sea-grass beds, but not in the open water.

SWORDFISH

The swordfish gets its name because its long extended upper jaw looks like a sword. The jaw makes up nearly a quarter of its body length. Swordfish are among the fastest swimmers of all the large fish. Scientists believe that swordfish stun their prey either with **shockwaves** created by the sword or by hitting the prey.

COMMON CUTTLEFISH

Common cuttlefish have a hard internal shell called a cuttle. When the fish dies, the cuttle washes up on beaches and people collect it for use in bird cages. Small groups of cuttlefish are found around rocky ledges and reefs. The cuttlefish changes color, from black to bright blue and green. Cuttlefish have grasping tentacles, like squid, that they use to catch their prey.

▶ Cuttlefish change color.

Deep Ocean

DEEP ABYSS

Light does not reach the deep abyss. Scientists have only recently begun to discover the animals that live here. Many of these animals produce their own light to attract prey or warn off predators. Strange-looking animals with large mouths or lures that dangle above gaping mouths are found in this cold, dark place.

▲ LANTERN FISH

The lantern fish family includes about 250 species. Lantern fish have organs on their bodies that give off light. They also have very good eyesight. These fish eat plankton, which they follow to the surface as night falls. They can then see the plankton in the murky light that filters through the water surface at night.

▶ The giant squid has never been seen swimming in its habitat.

▲ DEEP-SEA SQUID

There are a number of types of deep-sea squid, varying in shape and size from very small to the giant squid. The deep ocean bed is rich with food, and the squid are found in areas teeming with plankton, small fish, and shellfish.

▶ The megamouth shark has a large gulping mouth filled with small teeth.

▲ COOKIE-CUTTER SHARK

The cookie-cutter shark is one of the smallest sharks, less than one foot (30 cm) long. The cookie-cutter shark uses its sharp teeth and strong suction lips to bite and attach itself to larger animals such as megamouth sharks, whales, and large tuna. They leave behind a circular, cookie-shaped scar on the animal.

▶ The bite of a cookie-cutter shark is shaped like a cookie.

▶ DEEP-SEA CORAL

Scientists recently discovered corals living in the dark depths of the oceans in cold waters around 37°F (3°C). These deep-sea corals are very slow growing and live in tiny colonies on the seabed.

▲ GIANT SQUID

Giant squid measuring up to 52 feet (16 m) in length wash up on tropical beaches. No one has ever seen a giant squid swimming free in the ocean. They are thought to live in the dark depths of the open ocean.

◄ MEGAMOUTH SHARK

Only a few megamouth sharks have ever been found. Megamouth sharks have about 50 rows of very small teeth, but feed by filtering plankton, in the same way as the basking shark. It is thought that this species comes to the surface at night and then dives to about 500 feet (150 m) during the daytime.

► TINY COPEPODS
A copepod is a small crustacean. Crustaceans, such as shrimp, have hard, segmented shells. The tiny deep-sea copepods are plankton animals and exist in trillions in the depths of the ocean. They provide food for fish and squid. Surface-dwelling copepods include krill.

► COMMON EEL LARVAE
Common, or European, eel larvae have a flat, leaf-shaped body. A common eel larva is shown below, from right to left, in three stages of its development.

▲ SNIPE EEL

Some species in the deep abyss are "sit-and-wait" predators. These animals evolved in ways that allow them to wait for their prey to come to them. The snipe eel has a curved mouth and hook-like teeth. It uses these to catch the long antennae of passing shrimp.

► DEEP SEA GOOSEBERRY JELLYFISH
The gooseberry jellyfish, or sea gooseberries, are different from other jellyfish. They have small hairs that they wave back and forth to move through the water. Gooseberry jellyfish do not have stinging cells in their tentacles like other jellyfish. Their bodies are see-through and shaped like Christmas decorations. They are also known as comb jellies.

◄ OARFISH

The oarfish looks like a ribbon, with its long, narrow body that grows to 20 feet (6 m) long. The oarfish has a colorful set of dorsal fins. The first few fins stand up high above the others, like a crown, while the rest run down the back of the fish. Early sailors' stories of sea serpents might have been describing the oarfish.

▲ Its big eyes help the oarfish to spot its prey.

▼ GREENLAND SHARK

The deepest part of the ocean is very cold, with water temperatures of 35 to 37°F (2 to 3°C). Species of shark that inhabit these deep waters are used to the cold. One of the so-called sleeper sharks, the Greenland shark has been seen underneath **ice-floes** in the Arctic Ocean.

▲ The "sleepy" eye of a Greenland shark.

▲ GULPER EEL

Plants and animals have **evolved** in ways that allow them to survive in the environment in which they live. The ribbon-like gulper eel cannot see its prey in the dark depths of the ocean, so it has developed a large, gaping mouth. This helps it to trap passing prey and reduce the risk of missing an opportunity to eat.

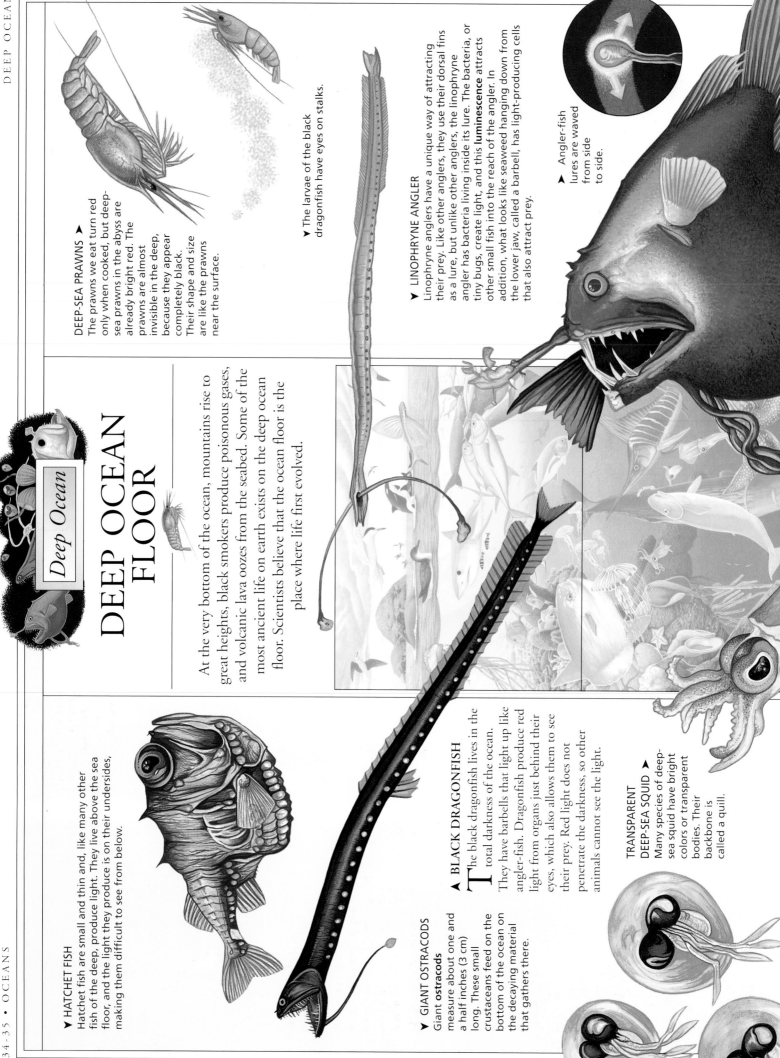

Deep Ocean

DEEP OCEAN FLOOR

At the very bottom of the ocean, mountains rise to great heights, black smokers produce poisonous gases, and volcanic lava oozes from the seabed. Some of the most ancient life on earth exists on the deep ocean floor. Scientists believe that the ocean floor is the place where life first evolved.

DEEP-SEA PRAWNS ▶
The prawns we eat turn red only when cooked, but deep-sea prawns in the abyss are already bright red. The prawns are almost invisible in the deep, because they appear completely black. Their shape and size are like the prawns near the surface.

▶ The larvae of the black dragonfish have eyes on stalks.

▶ **LINOPHRYNE ANGLER**
Linophryne anglers have a unique way of attracting their prey. Like other anglers, they use their dorsal fins as a lure, but unlike other anglers, the linophryne angler has bacteria living inside its lure. The bacteria, or tiny bugs, create light, and this **luminescence** attracts other small fish into the reach of the angler. In addition, what looks like seaweed hanging down from the lower jaw, called a barbell, has light-producing cells that also attract prey.

▶ Angler-fish lures are waved from side to side.

▶ **HATCHET FISH**
Hatchet fish are small and thin and, like many other fish of the deep, produce light. They live above the sea floor, and the light they produce is on their undersides, making them difficult to see from below.

▲ **BLACK DRAGONFISH**
The black dragonfish lives in the total darkness of the ocean. They have barbells that light up like angler-fish. Dragonfish produce red light from organs just behind their eyes, which also allows them to see their prey. Red light does not penetrate the darkness, so other animals cannot see the light.

▶ GIANT OSTRACODS
Giant **ostracods** measure about one and a half inches (3 cm) long. These small crustaceans feed on the bottom of the ocean on the decaying material that gathers there.

TRANSPARENT
DEEP-SEA SQUID ▶
Many species of deep-sea squid have bright colors or transparent bodies. Their backbone is called a quill.

VENT LIFE

Scientists were amazed at the amount and variety of life found around deep-sea vents when they were first discovered. Around these vents, minerals are spewed out of chimney stacks. These minerals support millions of bacteria, and feeding on the bacteria are fish, crab, shrimp without eyes, and giant **tubeworms** that grow to ten feet (3 m) long.

▶ The ocean floor is the **earth's crust**, and sometimes **superheated water** seeps out of cracks, creating black smokers.

▲ **Vent communities** consist mainly of tubeworms (top), as well as vent fish (above) and vent crab (top left).

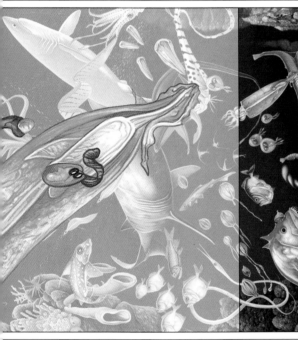

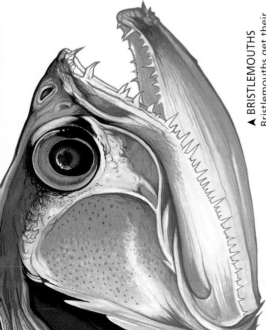

▲ DEEP-SEA BRITTLE-STARS
The deep-sea brittle-star is a starfish. They move their gangly arms across the seabed until they find something to wrap their long tentacles around. They then wait to capture any food that drifts by.

DEEP-SEA JELLYFISH ▶
Deep-sea jellyfish are hard, unlike soft surface jellyfish. Deep-sea jellyfish withstand greater pressure, because of the weight of water on their bodies. They produce light, which they use to confuse predators.

▲ BRISTLEMOUTHS
Bristlemouths get their name from the tiny hair-like teeth along the outer edge of their mouths. This group of fish are one of the most numerous of all fish in the ocean. Unlike many deep-sea fish, bristlemouths swim to hunt prey.

▼ HOLBOELL'S DEEP-SEA ANGLER
Angler-fish are sensitive to the tiniest movements to help them survive in the darkness. Holboell's deep-sea anglers have one or more hairy rods sticking out from their bodies that detect movement. Angler-fish sit and wait for fish, just like a fisher, or human angler. The female is over three feet (1 m) long. The male is smaller, about six inches (15 cm) long.

▶ The male angler (right) attaches himself to the female.

Deep Ocean

KEY TO FOLD-OUT

Use these key numbers if you want to identify the animals on the Deep Ocean fold-out. Most of them are featured on pages 28-35, and they are listed here in bold type. Animals that are not featured are also keyed and listed here, with a brief description.

1 White-Headed Petrel
The white-headed petrel is a small bird with a hooked beak that it uses to catch shellfish.

2 Bryde's Whale

3 Forster's Tern
The Forster's tern has a white crown in winter, which makes it look like it is wearing a black mask.

4 Killer Whale

5 Band-Rumped Storm-Petrel
The band-rumped storm-petrel can be seen flying over the ocean, but it nests on rocky islands.

6 Flying-Fish
Flying-fish do not fly, but they glide as much as 330 feet (100 m) or more across the ocean's surface. They build up speed underwater and then glide 20 inches (50 cm) above the surface to escape predators.

7 Northern Gannet

8 Anchovy

9 Yellow-Fin Tuna
Yellow-fin tuna is fast-swimming and has soft yellow fins. It lives in large schools and dives to 660 feet (200m).

35 Jewfish
The enormous jewfish is found in coastal waters. It vibrates a thin membrane to produce a very loud, thunderous sound.

36 Common Cuttlefish

37 Sea Urchin (red)
The red sea urchin was discovered when scientists discovered deep-sea corals. It has long, sharp spines.

38 Deep-Sea Coral

39 Ratfish
Ratfish are slow swimmers of the very deep ocean. They are distant relatives of sharks and rays.

40 Common Eel (larvae)

41 Oarfish

42 Giant Squid

43 Greenland Shark

44 Deep-Sea Squid

45 Deep-Sea Jellyfish
Deep-sea jellyfish come in a variety of sizes and shapes. Many are transparent, and some produce light.

46 Gulper Eel

47 Megamouth Shark

48 Lantern Fish

49 Diretmus
The diretmus is a small fish that lives in vast shoals close to rock faces.

50 Snipe Eel

51 Deep-Sea Gooseberry Jellyfish

52 Cookie-Cutter Shark

53 Tiny Copepods

54 Rat-Tail Fish
Rat-tail fish are the **scavengers** of the seabed. They gather in large groups to feed on carcasses that sink to the bottom.

55 Transparent Deep-Sea Squid

56 Giant Ostracods

57 Transparent Hatchet Fish
The transparent hatchet fish has a light lure inside its mouth. It also has eyes that see better looking up than down.

58 Holboell's Deep-Sea Angler
59 Hatchet Fish
60 Sea Lily
Sea lilies are filter-feeding animals. They have stalks that anchor them to the seabed while their branch-like arms capture passing plankton.
61 Holboell's Deep-Sea Angler
62 Deep-Sea Angler
The deep-sea angler has an expandable stomach and can eat fish twice its size. The backward-curving teeth make sure that nothing gets out.
63 Deep-Sea Prawn
64 Linophryne
65 Bristlemouth
66 Vent Crab
67 Vent Fish
68 Tubeworms
69 Deep-Sea Anomuran
Several different species of anomurans live on the deep seabed. The deep-sea anomuran looks like a cross between a lobster and a spider crab.
70 Sea Urchin (black)
Sea urchins have adapted to many different water environments. Familiar animals of shallow waters, they are also found on the deepest ocean floor and around deep sea vents. The ones shown without spines are the shells of dead sea urchins.
71 Deep-Sea Brittle-Star
72 Deep-Sea Rat-Tail
The bottom of the ocean is very dark, so some fish species have developed amazing senses. The deep-sea rat-tail, also known as the hollowsnout, has sense organs in its head to feel other fish that are around it.
73 Black Dragonfish
74 Deep-Sea Jellyfish

10 Long-Fin Tuna
11 Mako Shark (Short-Fin)
12 Greater Shearwater
13 Portuguese Man-of-War
14 Black-Jack
Black-jacks are night-feeding fish that live alone.
15 Krill
16 Pilotfish
The small pilotfish eats scraps and parasites from larger fish such as rays and sharks. In return, it does not get eaten by the larger fish.
17 Palometa
18 Crevalle Jack
19 Risso's Dolphin
20 Swordfish
21 Compass Jellyfish
22 Ocean Sunfish
23 Brittle-Star
Fossils of prehistoric brittle-stars have been found.
24 Splitlure Frogfish
25 Trumpet Sponge
26 Goose-Foot Star
The goose-foot star is a small species of starfish that is found as deep as 2,000 feet (600 m).
27 Atlantic Torpedo Ray
28 Atlantic Cuttlefish
The Atlantic cuttlefish has tentacles around its mouth. It is also found in shallow waters.
29 Pygmy Sperm Whale
30 Squid
Squid inhabit shallow water reefs. They have cells that allow it to change color instantly.
31 Leatherback Turtle
32 Sperm Whale
33 Atlantic Pipefish
34 Red Sponges
Sponges are one of the oldest animals on the planet, and come in many shapes and colors.

OCEANS

— GLOSSARY —

abyss Deep water below 3,300 feet (1,000 m)

algae Simple plant life

anemone Marine flowering plants that have brightly colored, buttercup-like flowers

bacteria Tiny, one-celled organisms

bait ball A large group of small fish grouped into a ball shape

baleen Thin, stiff material that hangs in the mouth of some whales and is used to filter food from water

black smoker A chimney-like structure around deep-sea vents through which hot gases from superheated water under the seabed escape

camouflage The natural coloring of an animal that allows it to blend in with its surroundings

canyon A deep, steep-sided split in the ground or the seabed

carcass The body of a dead animal

cells The smallest living unit of a plant or animal

colonies Groups of plants or animals of the same species living together

continental slope The area where the seabed drops from the shallow waters of the coastal area to between 650 and 6,500 feet (200 and 2,000 m)

coral A group of animals that produce a chalky outer skeleton and then live inside it, extending tentacle-like polyps to catch their food. Coral reefs are large structure made up of millions of coral animals all growing together

courtship The behavior of animals before mating

dorsal fin A fin that is on the upper surface of a fish or mammal

earth's crust The hard outer layer of the earth

echolocation Sound echoes produced and received by some animals to find food and other objects

evolve To gradually change over a long period of time

family A classification of similar species of plants and animals

fin A muscular structure like a flattened arm or leg that sticks out from a fish or mammal and used to move in water

food chain A series of animals or plants each depending on the next for food.

fronds The leaves of plants

gill slit The slits behind the head of fish that contain the gills

hot vents Splits in the earth's crust that allow very hot gases to escape

ice-floe A sheet of floating ice.

internal organs The parts inside a body that perform a specific function

kelp Any of several species of large seaweeds with flattened leaves

larvae A stage of growth in some animals before the adult stage

luminescence Production of light without heat

molt Replacement of one year's fur or feathers with new ones

nesting grounds The location of a bird's nest that is returned to each year to produce offspring

northern hemisphere The area to the north of the equator

nutrient A substance that provides nourishment for plants and animals

oceanic crust The surface of earth under the water

ostracods Small hard-shelled animals with many legs, such as crab, lobster, and shrimp

parasite An animal or plant that lives and feeds on another animal or plant while it is still alive

pectoral fin A fin that originates from the chest area of the animal

plankton Animals and plants that live in the sea and, unable to swim, travel around on the ocean currents

polyps Tentacle-like growths used by corals to catch food

prawn A crustacean similar to a shrimp, only larger

predators Animals that hunt and kill other animals for food

prehistoric Describes something from the time before written records were kept

ray A group of flat fish from the same family as sharks

scavenger Animals that hunt for dead animals or what remains of them, often stealing meat from other animals

school A group of whales, dolphins, or fish

sea urchin A small marine animal that has a flattened spiny shell

seabed The floor of the sea or ocean

shoal A large group of fish

shockwaves Strong waves produced by an abrupt motion

sponge A group of animals that remain motionless on the seabed and have an absorbent body with numerous holes in it

starfish A type of marine animal with five or more arms coming out of a central body

streamlined An object that is shaped to allow it to pass easily through air or water

superheated water Water that is heated beyond boiling point by hot volcanic lava beneath the seabed

tentacles Long and flexible arms of an animal used for moving, feeling, and catching prey

tissue A mass of similar cells that make up a body part

tropics The warm areas located near the equator

tubeworms Species of worms that live inside a hard, outer tube-shaped shell

vent communities Groups of animals and plants that live around deep-sea vents

volcanic islands Islands created by volcanic eruptions

—— INDEX ——